This Book
BELONGS TO

____

____

____

COLOR THIS PAGE

COLOR THIS PAGE

COLOR THIS PAGE

COLOR THIS PAGE

COLOR THIS PAGE

COLOR THIS PAGE

COLOR THIS PAGE

COLOR THIS PAGE

COLOR THIS PAGE

COLOR THIS PAGE

COLOR THIS PAGE

COLOR THIS PAGE

COLOR THIS PAGE

COLOR THIS PAGE

COLOR THIS PAGE

COLOR THIS PAGE

COLOR THIS PAGE

COLOR THIS PAGE

COLOR THIS PAGE

COLOR THIS PAGE

COLOR THIS PAGE

COLOR THIS PAGE

COLOR THIS PAGE

COLOR THIS PAGE

COLOR THIS PAGE

COLOR THIS PAGE

COLOR THIS PAGE

COLOR THIS PAGE

COLOR THIS PAGE

COLOR THIS PAGE

COLOR THIS PAGE

COLOR THIS PAGE

COLOR THIS PAGE

COLOR THIS PAGE

COLOR THIS PAGE

HEY, WE WANT TO HEAR FROM YOU!

PLEASE LEAVE A REVIEW BECAUSE WE WOULD LOVE TO KNOW YOUR THOUGHT'S

thanks for your support

thank
you

www.ingramcontent.com/pod-product-compliance
Lightning Source LLC
Chambersburg PA
CBHW081953260726
48657CB00009BA/2780